# SILK
paper

# SILK paper

## A GUIDE TO MAKING IT AND USING IT IN TEXTILE ART

Sarah Lawrence

**NORTH LIGHT BOOKS**

CINCINNATI, OHIO

**www.mycraftivity.com**

First published in North America
by North Light Books
an imprint of F+W Publications, Inc.
4700 East Galbraith Road
Cincinnati, OH 45236
800-289-0963

Photography and styling by **Sussie Bell**
Design by **Elizabeth Healey**

Conceived and produced by
Breslich & Foss Ltd.,
Unit 2A, Union Court,
20–22 Union Road,
London SW4 6JP

Library of Congress Cataloging-in-
Publication data available upon
request.

ISBN-13: 978-1-60061-117-9
ISBN-10: 1-60061-117-6

First published in Great Britain in
2008 by A&C Black Ltd.

Printed in China

10 9 8 7 6 5 4 3 2 1

# CONTENTS

# INTRODUCTION

The Chinese guarded the secret of sericulture, or silk making, for many centuries, and so there has always been an air of intrigue, secrecy, and romance surrounding silk. Its softness, luster, and its association with luxury and opulence all add to its mystique. My own interest in silk was captured early on in childhood by a box of my mother's beautifully colored silk threads. They remain to this day in their box–unused because they were silk and deemed too precious to disturb. Happily, over the last twenty years, silk fibers and silk cloth have become less expensive and more readily available, so that silk is no longer the preserve of those with wealth. It has become an affordable medium for textile artists.

I first came across silk fibers and their uses as a felt maker many years ago, and I am grateful to Joan Braganza who organized a weekend of workshops I attended where Inge Evers demonstrated a method of making silk paper. This started me on my journey to develop my own style of working with silk fibers of various types, incorporating them into contemporary textile work.

**Above** Pieces of silk paper can be further embellished with hand and machine stitches, beading and tassels, as demonstrated here.

I am personally interested in the wider story behind the materials that I use. Just as I like to know where the fibers for my feltmaking come from, I am interested in the historical and ethnographic context of silk fibers as well. I am fascinated by the early history of silk production and how it came to England, by the mistakes and successes made by kings and governments over centuries in order to establish the cultivation of silk and the development of a silk weaving industry,

and how the early English settlers in America were encouraged to rear silk worms.

The ability to construct a fabric gives the creative textile artist great freedom to develop a personal style. There is the possibility of total artistic control over the process, from the selection of fibers and the coloring of the silk to the choice of technique, and these are decisions that can dramatically alter the path of creativity.

I like to dye my own silk fibers–I get a real delight from the myriad of colors that are created from simple dye processes. I like the variety of textures and types of silk fiber that are available. I like the juxtaposition of luster, texture and the softness of silk. This is the reason for this book: to give an insight to those who have also been captivated and delighted by the lure of a very thin filament produced by a rather plump caterpillar. I hope that the information contained in this book allows you to develop your own silk style and to get the same amount of enjoyment and artistic satisfaction as I do in creating textile art from silk fibers.

# WORKING WITH
# SILK

This chapter contains the information you will need about the different types of raw silk from which silk paper can be constructed. There is also information on dyeing silk fibers.

# Silk Types

All silk comes from the same source: a cocoon produced by a silk worm. However, many factors affect the type and quality of silk that is produced, not least of which is the species of moth. *Bombyx mori* feeds only on the leaves of the mulberry bush and produces mulberry silk, which is white. Other moth species feed on other plants, which will affect the color and quality of the silk filament they produce.

Tussah silk is produced by wild silk moths that feed on different foodstuffs and produce a caramel-colored, very slightly rougher silk fiber. As the silk moth is allowed to emerge from the cocoon, breaking the continuous filament in the process, the cocoons cannot be reeled or "thrown" as with mulberry silk.

How the cocoons are processed will also affect the quality of the end product which, in the commercial world, is silk thread. There are two principal methods of silk thread production: silk reeling from whole cocoons and manufacture from pierced, cut or damaged cocoons. Fortunately for the creative textile artist, these processes produce by-products and it is these by-products that are used in this book.

## THE SILK PRODUCTION PROCESS

Silk reeling is the process by which silk thread is unwound from whole, intact, cocoons that have been softened in hot water. The aim is to draw off filaments that are as long as possible. This gives great strength to the thread that is produced. A number of cocoons are unwound simultaneously with several filaments joined together to form a single thread. As these are still very fine, two or three of these are twined together and reeled onto a skein. This silk filament still retains some gum, hence its name, "gummy filament."

One by-product of reeling is the carrier rod, which is made up of silk fiber that builds up on rods over which the silk is drawn. Periodically the rods are cut off to create carrier rod waste. Like cocoons, rods are sold by weight or by piece by the suppliers listed at the end of the book.

Not all the silk filament in a cocoon can be successfully drawn off as a continuous filament; leftover or broken threads are known as throwster's waste, and are another useful by-product for the textile artist. Like rods and cocoons, throwster's waste is gummy, but is often degummed by later processing.

Silk tops and sliver are produced from the remains of the cocoon when as much filament as possible has been extracted. Top is a form of silk in which long fibers are processed into parallel alignment. Top is generally sold by weight in a continuous length, but sometimes it is sold as a "brick," a knotted bundle weighing around 5 oz [150g]. Silk sliver is a thinner version of top that is usually sold by weight. Noil is a by-product of silk top production, and consists of short, very light fibers. Noil is sold by weight and 1 to 2 oz (30 to 50g) is adequate to begin with.

An alternative production method is used on pierced cocoons (where the moth has emerged) or cut, damaged or double cocoons (where two cocoons have been spun too close together and

## Tussah silk

Most commercially produced silk requires the stifling of the pupating moth in order to prevent the damage that the adult moth makes emerging from the cocoon. For those with ethical concerns, tussah silks are an alternative, as the moth emerges before the cocoons are gathered. Which silk to use is a personal, ethical decision and you should research this subject more thoroughly.

**Above** The silk types shown here are (from left to right and top to bottom): silk hankies, cocoon strippings, raw cocoons, mulberry silk sliver; gummy throwster's waste, degummed throwster's waste, tussah silk sliver; silk noil, mawata caps, rods.

become inseparable). Because of the damage, the fibers are shorter in length. To process these, the cocoons are first boiled in water to remove the gum (sericin) and make them soft. They are then turned inside out individually to remove pupae and other waste. Several cocoons are stacked and then spread by hand. These are then hung on a frame. They are then finished by washing and drying. The end result is silk caps or bells from which spun silk

can be produced. Tops and sliver can also be produced in the same way.

Thus, the way in which cocoons are handled results in different fiber types and forms. Some of these forms (such as the cocoons themselves and carrier rods), require a degree of preparation by the textile artist. Other silk types, such as caps and hankies, can be used with minimal preparation. The most useful preparation methods for cocoons, rods, hankies, and caps are shown on pages 12 to 21. Later in the book (pages 110–123), you'll find projects that use cocoons and rods in their unprocessed form.

## Sericin

Any silk that has "gum-in" or "gummy" in its name (for example, gummy throwster's waste) still contains a natural gum called sericin that binds the silk fibers to each other in the cocoon. Sericin is usually removed during the silk production process. Forms of silk that contain the gum are cocoon strippings, carrier rods and, of course, cocoons. Gummy silk types are used to make silk using the iron method on page 32.

Silk types that have had the gum removed are used in the medium method (page 68) and the stitched method (page 94). These silk types are mulberry and tussah tops, sliver, hankies, and caps. More processed forms such as condenser waste can also be used.

# Silk cocoons

A silk cocoon is the result of the process undertaken by the silk worm (the larval form of the *Bombyx mori* or silk moth) to create a protective environment while it pupates from a larva to a moth. The process begins when the caterpillar (the silk worm) has reached its maximum size, has eaten as much as it can, and is ready to pupate. It begins to produce a fluid that sets to become a silk filament and is continuous in length. The silk worm needs a vertical support to create the cocoon. In nature this would be a bush but in sericulture (silk production) straw and wood framing is used. The creation of the cocoon takes a couple of days. If the moth is allowed to mature naturally it produces a chemical that dissolves the gum surrounding the silk filament—the sericin—and emerges. However, a broken cocoon is not suitable for reeling so the moth is stifled within the cocoon, which allows for a

**Above** Here you can see three types of cocoons. (Top) Cut cocoons are usually not the best quality because of their irregular and nobbly shapes. They are sold in their natural state and can be dyed. (Middle) Golden cocoons are very rare, delicate, and lacey. (Bottom) These whole cocoons contain the stifled moth larvae.

**Below** Stretched cocoons have a wonderful texture that can be put to good use in decorative projects.

continuous filament to be reeled off. Broken or damaged cocoons are generally used for spinning; a spun silk is produced in the same way as a woolen or cotton yarn. Whole cocoons, which tend to be more evenly shaped, are all approximately 2 in. (5 cm) in size.

A good mulberry silk cocoon can produce more than 400 yards of continuous silk filament. When preparing cocoons it is important to remove the outside layer of silk waste (this is loose fiber). The innermost layer (the envelope), like the skin on a peanut, is also waste. Dupion silk is a spun silk fabric made from double cocoons—irregular shapes that give the fabric its distinctive texture. Silk cocoons can be bought by weight or by piece, and in a natural or undyed state.

The softening and stretching preparation method shown here allows the fibers to be spun out later.

1 Select some whole cocoons and remove any loose waste fibers from their outside to leave the cocoon smooth. (The waste can be used for compost material.) With a sharp pair of scissors, pierce the outer shell and cut through the cocoon to reveal the stifled remains of the silk moth pupa. Discard.

**YOU WILL NEED:**

• whole cocoons

• small, sharp scissors

• bowl

• tweezer

2 Place the cut and emptied cocoons into a bowl of very hot water and allow them to soak. The cocoons will sink and go translucent when the water has penetrated the fiber layers. This will soften and disrupt the sericin gum surrounding the silk fibers, which will allow them to be stretched and split. You may find that adding a drop of washing-up liquid will assist in the soaking process.

3 Use tweezers to remove the softened cocoons from the bowl, as they may still be hot. Use pliers to begin pulling the cocoon apart; as the material cools, you will be able to use your fingers. The cocoon can be stretched to create a very distinctive sheet. After a while it will become difficult to pull and stretch the silk because the sericin that was softened by the hot water will begin to set again. At this point you can repeat the softening process described in Step 2 if necessary.

4 Continue to stretch the cocoon to create a textured fabric that can be utilized in many projects.

# Rods

Carrier rod waste is formed over a metal rod in the reeling process. The rods themselves are stick-like in shape and generally about 6 in. (15 cm) long. As the silk waste builds up on the rod during the silk production process, it is sliced away to keep the rod clean. The resulting waste is very hard and laden with sericin. The rods themselves can be used as structural items just as they are, or they can be cut and dyed. In this example I used dyed rods. A useful way to incorporate rods into textile pieces is to separate the layers into thin sheets of silk fiber. Carrier rod waste can be bought by weight or by piece, and in a natural or undyed state.

1  Take a dyed or natural colored rod and open up the structure.

2  Bend the strip of silk back onto its spine and begin to curl the end back on itself.

3  Continue to curl the rod until a tight roll is formed.

**YOU WILL NEED:**

• rods in a natural or dyed state

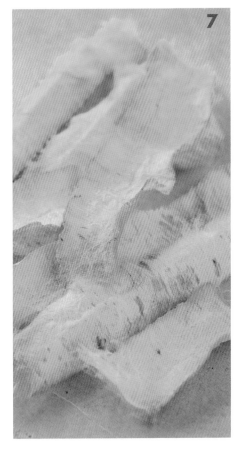

**4** Roll this silk mass between your hands several times until the fibers soften. The continuous movement and pressure from your hands will break the rigid structure created by the sericin gum.

**5** Open out the softened silk ribbon. You will notice that the edge has begun to separate into layers.

**6** Carefully peel away each layer.

**7** Some of the layers that you have separated will be complete; others will be short or broken. This really does not matter, as these pieces can be used as they are.

# Creating threads

1 To produce a thread, stretch out a single delaminated ribbon of silk.

2 You will notice that, as the ribbon of fiber is stretched out, a very distinctive lattice pattern emerges. These pieces can be used for decorative projects just as they are.

3 Take one end of the stretched silk ribbon and twist it to create a very decorative slubbed yarn.

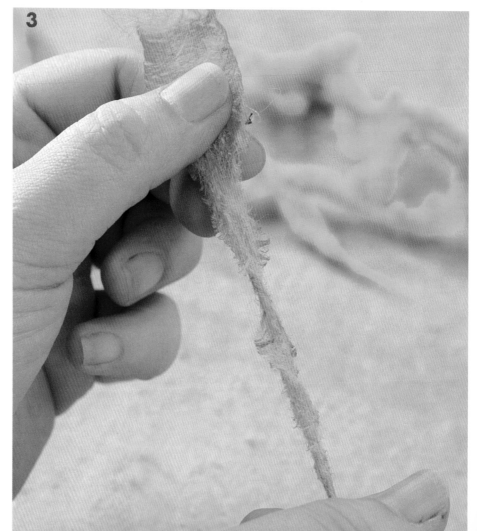

## TIP

A slubbed yarn, such as the thread made here, is an irregular or uneven yarn. Slubbed yarns can be used for decorative knitting or stitching.

**Top** Carrier rod waste in its undyed form.

**Above** Twisted carrier rod yarn ready for use in a project.

**Right** Thin layers taken from rose-colored rods can be rolled up to form silk roses.

# Silk hankies

Silk hankies are flat, stretched cocoons that are roughly square in shape and about 8 x 8 in. (20 x 20 cm): the size of a Victorian lady's handkerchief. Hankies are supplied in multilayered stacks because they are made from many cocoons. In one corner of the stack of layers there is a hole that marks the place where the edge of the softened cocoons was placed to allow purchase for the stretching process.

To utilize this silk form, look carefully at the edge of a stack of hankies and you will notice that each layer is reasonably identifiable. If you pull the dry layers apart slowly, they will be difficult to separate as the fibers cling together between the layers. Pull apart in one swift motion. When dyeing hankies, I like to separate them at the end of the process before they dry out because wet hankies are easier to separate.

Hankies can be used as they are to create silk paper, but they can also be used to create a yarn. Traditionally hankies are placed onto specialized spinning equipment and the fibers spun out. I have not yet fully mastered the art of spinning so the yarns that I create are textural rather than technically correct. I would advise anyone who is interested in

developing this method to draw on the experience of friends who are more accomplished in the art of spinning. It is relatively easy to set this up for drop spindling. Further ways to use silk hankies are described throughout the book.

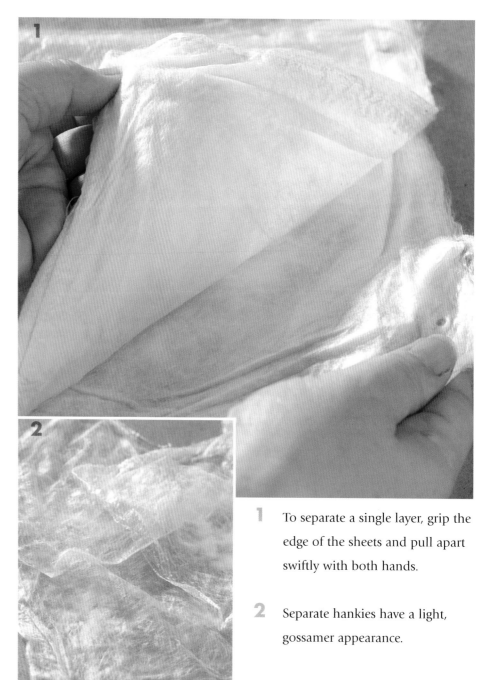

1  To separate a single layer, grip the edge of the sheets and pull apart swiftly with both hands.

2  Separate hankies have a light, gossamer appearance.

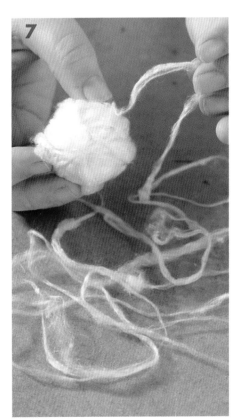

**3** Grasp a hankie in both hands and rip a hole in the center.

**4** Begin to pull apart the hankie.

**5** Break off a section of hankie from the inner ring.

**6** Begin to twist the yarn into a thread. To prevent it becoming knotted up, you may wish to roll the thread around a straw.

**7** Form the thread into a ball ready for a project (knitting).

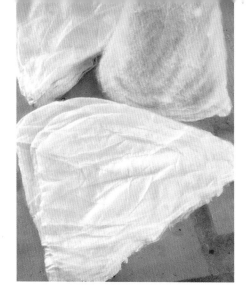

# Mawata caps

Mawata caps have a bell-like shape that is formed by workers opening out and stretching cocoons over a domed former. To prepare a silk yarn from stretched caps, you will need the assistance of another person.

1. Take the edge of the cap and stretch it into a square, making sure your partner has a firm grasp of the other end.

2. With one partner holding firmly onto the edge, the other partner should pull the cap toward themselves. The cap will be quite resistant, but eventually you will feel the silk fibers loosen and give way under pressure.

3. Both partners can now begin to stretch out the sheet of silk.

4. Continue to stretch out a rectangular shape, holding firmly onto the edges.

**5** Eventually you will create a very fine cobweb. This can then be elongated and stretched to form a continuous rope of silk.

**6** Twist gently to make a new silk thread that can be used for knitting or hand stitch work. If you are able to use a drop spindle or a spinning wheel, you will create a finer more consistent thread. Wind the newly created silk thread into a ball ready for use. You can do this by hand or use a mechanical ball winder. In my experience it is not necessary to ply two threads together for this very basic yarn. However, if you are able to find out more about conventional spinning and yarn making this will definitely improve your ability to make a consistent or creative yarn. With patience, enough yarn can be spun to produce a small knitted garment.

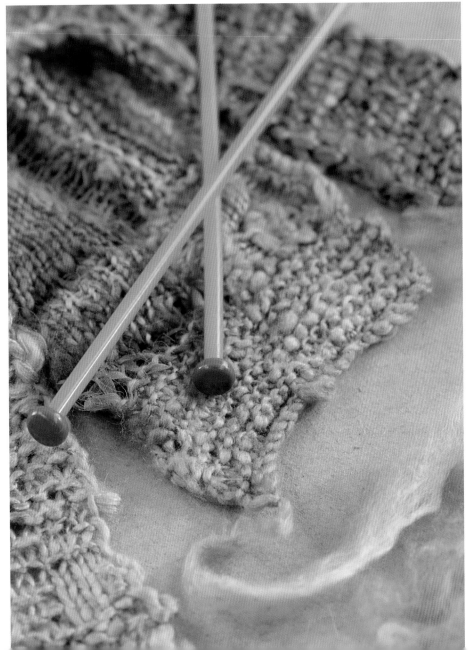

**Left** Samples of knitting made from stretched, dyed mawata caps. These were knitted on medium sized needles (chosen because they were pretty!). The knitted fabric has a pleasing slubbed or uneven surface. Knitted pieces like these can be incorporated into silk fabric using the iron method. (See pages 44 to 45.)

# Dyeing

Although the tone and texture of silk in its natural state is beautiful, you can also create a medley of colors by dyeing the silk. The luster and luminosity of dyed silk fibers are truly wonderful. The simple but effective dyeing methods described in the following pages will allow you to create your own color palette for the projects you have in mind. The way fibers are laid down in the various dyeing methods ensures that the different colors in the fibers will mingle with any silk that you dye, even when the fibers are layered on top of each other (unless the layers are very dense). The following methods of dyeing allow you to create a bold, bright, powerful palette should you wish, or an elegantly subtle display. Just remember, even when you have dyed your chosen silk fibers, if you are not completely satisfied with the color blends, then you can just over-dye them (repeat the dyeing process) to create new color blends.

It is always helpful to have a selection of dyed caps and hankies stored and ready for use in projects.

# Types of dye

There are various dyes available which are easy to use and need a minimum of equipment. The dyes I have used in this chapter are easily available, simple to use, and give very good results. Whether using acid or procion dyes, or the all-in-one liquid dyes that require steam or heat from a microwave, remember that you can mix colors within dye types to suit your particular project.

## Acid dyes

Acid dyes are used to color wool and other animal or protein fibers. Fibers such as silk and synthetics (nylon) are also dyed with these dyes. Acidic conditions are required to fix acid dyes. These are generally achieved by adding white vinegar or, in some cases ammonium sulphate crystals, to water.

### GUIDELINES FOR DYE-TO-FIBER WEIGHT

| DRY WEIGHT TO BE DYED | VINEGAR | WATER |
| --- | --- | --- |
| 1¾ oz (50g) | 1¾ fl oz (50ml) | 6½ cups (1.5 l) |
| 3½ oz (100g) | 3½ fl oz(100ml) | 12⅔ cups (3 l) |
| 7 oz (200g) | 7 fl oz(200ml) | 25⅓ cups (6 l) |

The above are only guidelines. As you gain experience in dyeing, you will find that you may use less dye, as the saturation of these dyes is strong.

### MAKING UP DYE STOCK

Feel free to alter the values of this basic recipe to suit the color strength needed for your projects.

#### YOU WILL NEED:

- clean containers (large drinking cups or similar or screw top jars)
- assorted acid dyes
- measuring spoons
- measuring cup
- wooden coffee stirrers

Measure 1¼ cups (300 ml) of liquid and add ⅛ tsp (63 ml) of acid dye powder. Mix with a wooden coffee stirrer or similar. It is important that each color has its own set of stirrers to avoid cross contamination of color. If not used all at once, this dye stock can be kept in an airtight/screw top jar for several months. Should the liquid evaporate, it can be revived with the addition of water. Note that these liquid to powder ratios are approximate, and you may want to adjust the color strength by adding a bit more, or a bit less, powder.

# Procion dyeing

Silk fiber and, indeed, other silk materials are unusual in that they can be dyed with acid dyes and procion dyes. Acid dyes are usually intended for animal protein materials, such as wool. Procion dyes are generally recognized as being suitable for plant materials or cellulose-based materials. I have not used procion dyeing in this book because it requires a more considered approach than acid dyeing. Generally, I would recommend that procion is best used by people who wish to dye large volumes of silk.

Procion dyes will only work when there is a high alkaline presence. This is why soda crystals are dissolved in water and added to the dye bath. This makes the dye reactive, and the salt solution encourages the dye to leave the water and interact with the materials being dyed. Always follow the manufacturer's instructions when using procion dyes.

# Rainbow dyeing

Before applying the dye, the silk must be prepared to accept it. To do this, place your chosen silk sliver in a large bowl containing a small amount of white vinegar to acidify the water. The acid in the vinegar will help to bind the dye to the silk fibers. Although there are lots of very precise recipes, I find that in a bowl containing approximately 6 pints (3 litres) of water, half a cup of white vinegar is sufficient. (Don't use darker malted vinegar as this is too pungent.) Leave the fibers to soak overnight or until they slightly swell and turn translucent. Check that there are no dry patches, as dry areas will not dye. Take your fibers out of the water and firmly wring them out. Don't be afraid to squeeze: silk fibers are incredibly

strong and you will see that the sliver rope remains intact.

If you choose to use mulberry silk sliver, the whiter fibers will offer a purer color; if tussah sliver is used, the darker fibers will enrich the color that is added to it.

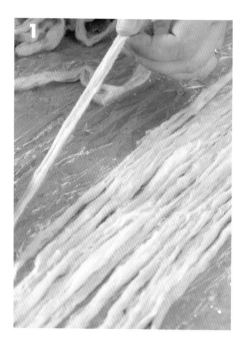

**1** On a suitable work surface, stretch out two layers of plastic wrap approximately 2 ft (60 cm) in length. Take the wetted fibers and lay them out in lines, leaving about 6 in. (15 cm) clear at either end of the plastic wrap.

**2** Taking your dye pots and sponge brush, sponge lines of dye across the width of the silk slivers by repeatedly dabbing and reloading the sponge brush with dye mix. This will create very clear areas of color.

**3** Continue to add lines of dye in a second color, using a new foam brush per dye pot. By adding blue, the red dye already applied will develop a purple line where the two colors meet.

## YOU WILL NEED:

- plastic wrap
- 1¾ oz (50 g) or more of silk sliver
  acid dyes
- foam brushes
- large bowl
- vinegar
- microwave
- latex or rubber gloves
- plate

4 When yellow is added, it will create green when it meets the blue dye and orange where it runs into the red. If you find the color is not as intense as you expected, add a few more grains of acid dye to the dye pots to make a stronger solution. Apply repeatedly to the sliver until you are happy with the color.

5 Very carefully roll up the plastic wrap like a Swiss roll.

6 Roll into a spiral and put it onto a microwave-proof dish. Place in a microwave oven and cook on the highest setting for two to three minutes. If you don't have a microwave, place the roll in a steamer and steam for half an hour. It is the heat-activated reaction between the dye, silk, and acid that fixes the color onto the surface of the silk.

7 Carefully remove the heated fibers from the microwave and open out the roll. Allow to cool. When cool, rinse the newly dyed fibers in warm water so that excess unwanted dye stock is removed. Rinse until the water is clear, then allow the fibers to dry.

**Right** Rainbow-dyed silk sliver that has been left to dry indoors.

# Microwave random dyeing

There are a number of liquid products available for dyeing silk. Most of these products contain both color and fixative and can be applied directly to wetted silk fibers. Please read individual manufacturer's instructions, as processing may vary slightly. These easily applied, all-in-one dyes are available in many colors and, like most other dye stuffs, can be mixed or blended to create unique color combinations.

Before dyeing, prepare the silk fibers by soaking them in warm water. You can also add a drop of washing-up liquid to accelerate the wetting process. When the fibers are thoroughly soaked, wring them out and place them in a shallow plastic container. In this project, I've used (top to bottom) sliver, condenser waste, and noil.

**YOU WILL NEED:**

- a selection of liquid color dyes
- a selection of silk fibers such as noil, condenser waste, and silk sliver
- shallow plastic container
- latex or rubber gloves

1  Squirt the first color randomly over the fibers.

2  Add the second and third colors, adjust the first if necessary. By using yellow, blue, and red, a myriad of colors will be achieved.

3  Squeeze up the fibers, keeping them in separate heaps.

4  Place in a microwave oven and cook on the highest setting for two to three minutes. After the color has been activated, the fibers should be rinsed until no excess color remains and the water runs clear. Allow the fibers to dry out before using them in a project.

# PROJECTS
## THE

## YOU WILL NEED:

- newspaper or newsprint
- heat resistance surface
- a roll or several sheets of non-stick baking parchment or similar
- approximately ½ oz (10g) of gum-in fibers, such as cocoon strippings, gummy throwster's waste or gummy filament
- spritzer bottle
- iron—either a travel sized one or an ordinary one

1   Lay out the cocoon strippings on the baking parchment. To do this, hold the bulk fiber in one hand and pull out small handfuls. The fibers are usually well aligned and can be pulled away in small drifts.

2   Lay out the fibers so they overlap each other on the sheet of baking parchment. You can lay them in neat rows (as shown here) or more randomly. If you want to end up with an evenly gauged silk paper then you will need to "tweak" the layers so they appear even.

3   To make a natural colored paper, simply spray cold water in a light mist over the fibers. Hold the spritzer about 8 in. (20 cm) above the surface of the fibers.

4   Place another piece of baking parchment on top of the pile of fibers.

5   Iron over the surface of the baking parchment with a medium to hot iron. (Do not use the steam setting.) You may hear a "sizzle" as the water mist is heated by the iron. This is normal! Iron methodically over the surface for a few seconds.

6   You can unpeel the baking parchment and the silk paper at this stage, which will be a little limp, and set it aside to dry and harden up.

TIP

The way in which you lay out the fibers will have an effect on how the finished paper looks. In this project, the fibers are laid out in regular lines. To create the effect of contrasting denser and thinner areas (where the fibers are fine enough to see through), lay the fibers out randomly instead. The more experience you have of pulling the fibers the more you will gain confidence in arranging them for the project you have in mind.

7   The back of the paper (shown here) is softer than the front.

8   If you don't want the delicate wispy edges that naturally occur, the edges can be folded over and ironed. If the silk paper is a little dry, lightly re-spritz where the fold will be. Fold the baking parchment over and iron along the crease. If you iron directly onto the newly formed silk paper, the iron will stick to it and spoil your work.

## TIP

To create a stronger paper (suitable for 3-D constructed pieces and projects that are going to have shapes cut or punched out of them or be stitched), flip the "sandwich" over in Step 6, peel the parchment from the back, and spritz the fibers lightly again with water. Replace the parchment and re-iron for a few seconds.

# Adding embellishments

I like to add lightweight natural additions to my papers, such as rose petals, dried flowers, leaves, autumnal seed cases, and sinamays (woven material made from banana fibers). These complement the style of the silk paper that the iron method creates.

1  Lay the natural things on the spritzed fibers in Step 3, cover with a few more fibers and spritz.

2  Cover with baking parchment and iron as you did in Steps 4 and 5. The sericin that the heat and moisture reactivates draws in these additions and "glues" them to the fibers.

3  Instead of folding over the edges and ironing, you can also trim the piece to size with scissors.

# Adding color

A simple and effective way to color the fibers is to use spray colorants instead of dyes. Although you can dye your own fibers beforehand using the microwave method or another method of your choice (see Dyeing, page 22), I have found this method of coloring to be fast, effective, and fun to do.

1 Spray on a combination of colorants directly (as shown) or through a stencil. Then place the baking parchment on top and iron.

2 If you want to add gold or metal flakes, sprinkle them on the fibers before ironing.

A colored paper with metallic highlights makes a lovely piece in itself, or can be further embellished or used in other projects.

**3** To enrich the color, flip the sandwich over and spritz a different color onto the back of the fibers. Replace the parchment and iron.

**4** Flip over the sandwich and peel back the baking parchment to reveal the color of the reverse side. Fold in the edges and carefully iron over the baking parchment.

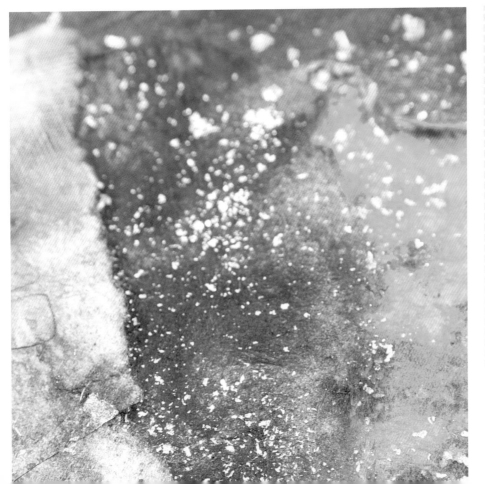

TIP

Color sprays, such as the ones used here, are widely available from craft stores. Found in matte, iridescent, and metallic varieties, they are generally used by paper crafters to color paper.

# Layering with sinamay

Natural products—such as sinamay—can be included in silk paper with the iron method. Sinamay is made from banana fibers and has a very open weave. It is used widely in hat-making. To integrate sinamay into a piece of silk paper, lay it over the unprocessed fibers and spray it with color or plain water, then iron as normal. The sinamay will be held in place by the gummy sericin in the silk fibers. The inlaid structure is ideal for further decoration and lends support to the construction of boxes and containers. A simple box can be created by folding, cutting, and assembling. The simplest way to make a pattern is by undoing and drawing around a gift bag.

**Above** In this sample, thin strips of silk paper were cut and interwoven over the sinamay surface. Then the piece was decorated with hand stitches as well as mother-of-pearl discs and beads.

**Left** To create this piece, I inserted a small section of openly woven sinamay between layers of cocoon strippings. The piece was then lightly colored with bronze and mauve sprays. When dry, I added small gold squares, painted in acrylic. Finally, I stitched separate backed squares of copper-colored silk paper onto the surface. The backing lifts the squares away from the flat surface of the silk both physically and visually. I then created free motion blocks around the golden squares. The pattern was then further embellished with copper-colored square sequins and multicolored bronze and blue iridescent beads.

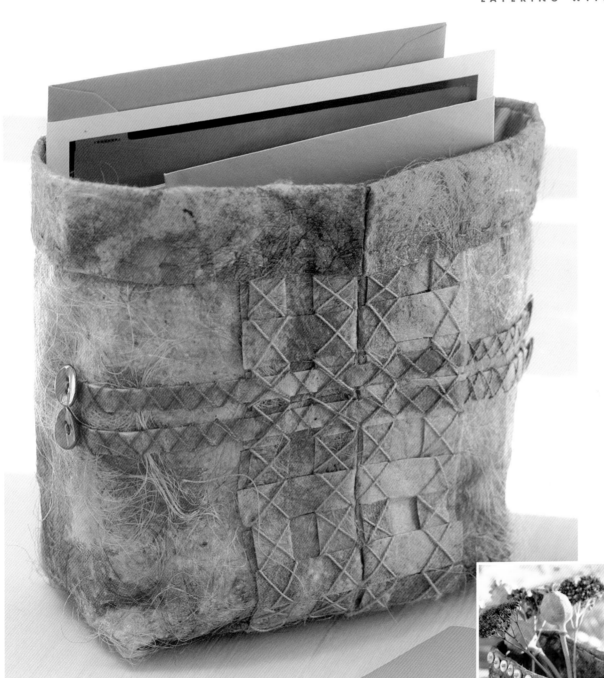

**Above** This container was made from a combination of silk filament and cocoon strippings, using the iron method. The simple box construction has a turn over top to show the contrast between the web-like surface of the outside (made by the silk filaments) and the smoother surface inside. Extra decoration was added with woven strips of silk paper with decorated with mother-of-pearl button and beads.

**Right** One piece of iron method silk paper with open-meshed sinamay incorporated into it was used to form this container, which was then embellished with simple hand stitches and mother-of-pearl buttons and beads. This piece is not lined, but a simple cloth lining could easily be made for it.

**Opposite** These silk flowers were made using the iron method, cut out with a template, and folded into shape. The background is iron method silk paper to which sinamay has been added.

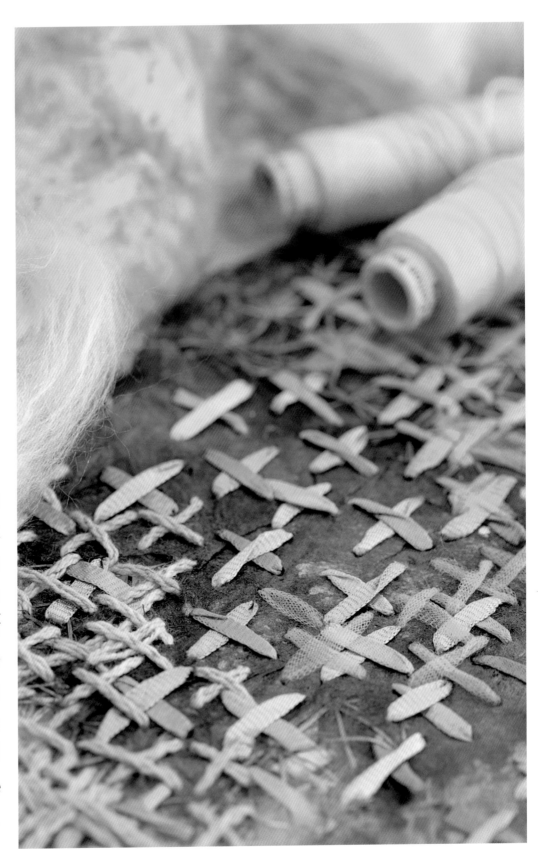

In this sample, a piece of silk paper was made with a layer of sinamay. The paper was then embellished with bold hand stitches to create texture.

## ADDING KNITTING

Create dynamic surfaces by laying knitted pieces onto gummy silk then ironing them as normal. Spray color will easily be taken up by natural fibers such as cotton, linen, and silk. This will result in an integrated and harmonious texture. Further enhancements can be made to the surface with hand or machine stitching, although the new fabric may need to be stabilized with a backing to prevent the different thicknesses of the surface from puckering when the machine stitch is applied. If knitting is not your strongest craft skill, don't worry; so long as the stitches are somehow connected, dropped stitches will add to the drama of the surface. Any loose stitches will be secured by the fusion of the silk to the natural knitted surface. If you can only purl and knit, use very large needles to create the open structure that is best suited for incorporation into a silk surface.

**Right** The interest in this piece is created by the contrast of strong texture with natural tones as the knit structure meets the smooth addition of silk fibers.

**Above** The knit structure in this piece uses a combination of knit and purl stitches only, creating texture and contrast which then interacts with the smoothness of the silk. Some fancy yarns were used, but the majority are cotton and silk.

**Right** The knitted element in this sample was created from dyed, spun mawata hankies (see page 18). The silk paper background was further enhanced with simple stitches to build up more texture and to create a graduated effect between the knitting and the silk paper.

# Heat embossing

Embossing with thermo-reactive powder is a lovely way to add a discrete motif to the surface of a piece of silk paper. There are many powders to choose from: fine grade powders create a smooth, low-relief effect. Larger crystals result in a more raised finish and a slightly "distressed" look, which adds character to a piece.

1   Tap the embossing ink onto the rubber stamp to get an even coverage. Stamp the image onto the silk.

2   Sprinkle the printed area with the embossing powder.

## YOU WILL NEED:

- heat-resistant surface
- embossing ink
- rubber stamp with an open design, found objects, corks, or home-made printing blocks
- sheet of dry silk paper made using the iron method
- embossing powder or crystals
- copy paper
- heat gun

**3**

**4**

**5**

**3** Tip the excess powder onto a piece of copy paper and replace it in its original container. Repeat Steps 1 to 3 until the embossed design is completed.

**4** Activate the embossing powder or crystals with the heat gun. Don't concentrate the heat on one area, instead distribute the heat evenly until all the granules have melted.

**5** You will notice that the granules melt and change under the heat.

**Left** A section of embossing has been cut to create an open design, which is then laid onto a silk background that is also embossed. A simple running stitch attaches both pieces together, and it is completed with the addition of small beads.

**Above** This shows a repeated image printed onto silk paper and then dusted with gold embossing powder.

# Molding

The rubber stamp or sheet you use in this process should be very clean, as any color on it may transfer to the silk. After a couple of uses, you will find that the rubber will be a little sticky because of the sericin that is released from the gummy silk fibers.

**1** Place a sheet of silicone paper on the work surface, then spray the surface of the rubber stamp with water or color spray. The liquid helps to create the molded silk, and also acts as a release agent.

**2** Place generous amounts of loose silk fiber onto the mold and spray on more color.

**3** Spray color generously over the top of the fiber pile.

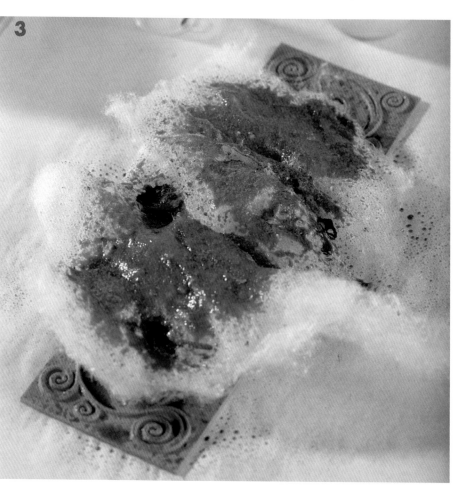

**YOU WILL NEED:**

- heat-resistant surface
- 2 sheets of silicone paper
- rubber stamp or molding sheet with an open or deeply etched design
- color spray of your choice, or water spray
- cocoon strippings
- iron

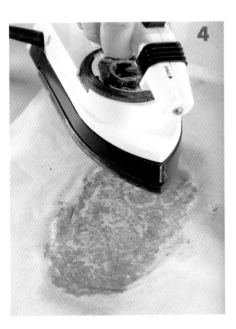

**4** Place the second silicone sheet over the fibers and, using a hot setting, iron the layers. As soon as you see the shadow of the mold appear, stop ironing.

**5** Quickly, and with a positive action, turn the mold over and remove the cast silk away from the mold. It is always best to remove the cast silk from the mold immediately, although please note that it may be quite warm to handle. However, if you leave it to cool, the sericin will harden, making it difficult to remove the cast effectively. Because a lot of liquid is used to color the silk, it can take a while to dry out. When the casts are dry they can be stitched, glued, and cut. The cast silk can also be enhanced by over-painting or patinating the surface with shoe polish or gilding waxes.

**Above** A collection of silk casts, waiting to be used in decorative projects.

**Above** This small molded panel has been overstitched and bound with machine stitching.

**Right** This textile panel incorporates cast silk motifs, beads, machine stitchery, and mother-of-pearl shapes. Some cast elements were cut away and used as single decorative motifs. Cast elements like these can be used to make small pieces of jewelry, such as brooches: simply cut to shape, line the back, and attach an appropriate fastener.

# Using dimensional paste

Adding a touch of luxury to the surface of silk papers with dimensional paste is simple to do and the results are elegant. Dimensional paste is a thick, viscose, gel-like material that is available in many types and colors. Other materials—such as fine glitter, accent beads, and gilding flakes—can be mixed into the paste before it is applied to add further interest.

1   Lay the stencil over the silk paper base. Tape around the edges of the stencil with low-tack tape to secure the stencil, and protect the edges.

2   Carefully remove the dimensional paste from the tub with a palette knife. Drag the paste over the stencil. Keep the palette knife at a low angle so that the paste is delivered evenly.

**YOU WILL NEED:**

• stencil, brass, or plastic (the deeper the stencil the more raised the result will be)

• piece of silk paper

• low-tack tape

• dimensional paste

• palette knife or a piece of stiff plastic

**3**

TIP

Even though the iron method was used for this particular project, most silk surfaces can be embellished with dimensional paste. Once you gain confidence in cutting your own stencils from plastic or cardboard, you will find the decorative potential of this particular process endless.

**Below** Because I used gummy throwster's waste for this sample, the resulting stencil is slightly "fuzzy" rather than crisp and clean.

**3** When the area of the stencil is filled, remove the tape and lift the stencil away with a confident movement. If you hesitate you may smudge the image. Remove the stencil before the paste dries, or it will stick to the fibers. If you don't intend to reuse it immediately, wash the stencil with warm soapy water and leave to dry. Once dry, the piece can be over-colored with patinating waxes, acrylic paints, and crafters' chalks, or embroidered.

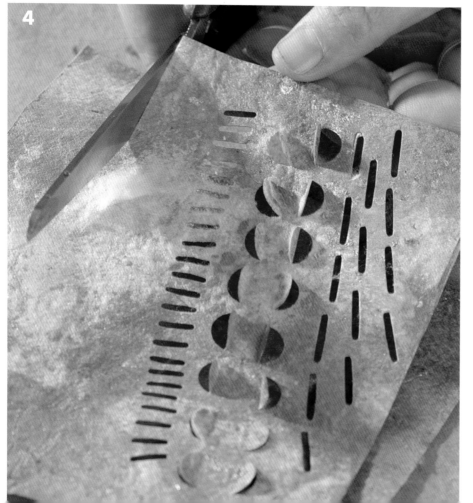

3    Cut further spaces using the slot and ribbon dies. The small pieces that are removed in the die-cutting process can be kept in a small pot and used as decorative elements in other projects.

4    Cut away a large border from the die-cut edge. Shape these edges using a half-moon cutter to form an arched or staggered wave effect. Choose a background paper in a contrasting color.

5    Thread a small ribbon of silk paper in and out of the slots created.

**Opposite** Arrange the die-cut sections on background paper chosen in Step 4. Place them so that the spaces and openings created with the die-cutting tools are shown to best effect: make sure there is a strong color where they appear. I developed this piece further with beads and hand stitching. The green elements on the finished item are Victorian foiled glass discs.

Simple slots laced with a contrasting strip of silk paper creates a wonderful detail for a book page or greeting card.

**Right** Half-moon and slot die tools were used to create this piece. The top surface was then decorated with embossing powders, sequins, and woven strips.

## LACÉ WORK

Sheets of silk paper made using the iron method are best for this decorative process, because the paper is crisp and easy to cut. The technique is probably Dutch in origin, but the word lacé is French and means laced or linked together. Use a sheet that is a different color or tone on each side, and remember that you can add light decorative elements, such as metal flake or threads, should you wish. (See page 39.) There are many metal templates for this decorative process, but it is far more fun to cut and fold back shapes that you have created yourself. For this you will need a sharp, fine-bladed craft knife or fine pointed scissors, a ruler, and a pencil.

Cut designs through the silk paper. Once all the slots or slits have been cut, the pattern pieces can be folded back. Lightly scoring the folds will help to create a much neater fold. The folded pieces can be layered over each other or simply interlocked. When you have cut and folded your pieces, you can decorate the multicolored and multilayered surface further with long hand stitches. If you are using a heavy thread, you may need to use a steel point (stiletto) or large gauged bodkin to make a pilot hole through the silk paper layers for the thread to pass through easily. Adding bugle beads of different

lengths can enhance the geometric quality of the surface pattern.

Because of the open structure of the patterns that are created, this type of work is delightful left as it is or backed with a contrasting fabric to create a picture or wall panel. Cutting unevenly, changing the direction of the cut, and cutting with sharp decorative scissors leads to endless creative possibilities. I would strongly recommend that you try out the cut pattern on paper before you do it on the silk paper: cut once measure twice!

Patterns are formed by cutting and folding silk sheets. All these pieces have been embellished with beads that secure the folded flaps and enhance the overall shapes.

## DECORATIVE FOLDING

This is a lovely way to create a simple book from one sheet of silk paper. It also allows for the addition of many decorative details. The doubled pages can be made into pockets by only sealing two rather than three edges. Apertures can be cut out to enable other flat decorative items to be framed.

Begin by making a large piece of silk paper using the iron method. The size you make will depend on the eventual page size you want. For example, a finished page size of 4 x 4 in. (10 x 10 cm) requires a minimum sheet size of 16 x 16 in. (40 x 40 cm) as the starting size; a page measuring 5 x 4 in. (13 x 10 cm) requires a sheet 20 x 16 in. (50 x 40 cm).

Following the template, mark and cut out a sheet the correct size. Draw fold lines onto the silk with a ruler and pencil. Each line should be folded and creased up and down several times (mountain and valley folds) to help in the assembly of the book. If you wish, you can make a decorative cover by measuring the size of the pages, adding the width of the spine, and cutting this shape out of silk paper (or indeed any other fabric). You may wish to support it with a lightweight material, such as Vilene. The book can be glued or stitched into position.

**Above** Use mountain and valley folds to create a simple book out of a piece of silk paper.

**Opposite** You can glue or sew a decorative cover onto your book.

# Making a book

Highly embellished sheets of silk paper look lovely bound together to make books. Here, I added paper flowers and metallic flakes to silk fibers after they were sprayed with color and before they were ironed. Ironing makes the extra elements adhere to the surface. The papers were then left to dry. Each paper was further decorated with paint, stitching, and embellishments such as tin leaves, ribbons, and lace. Once all the surface embellishments had been added, I sandwiched interlining material (cut slightly smaller than the silks) between the papers. I stitched some of these sandwiches together by hand with running stitch or more complicated stitches, such as knotted button hole to create an edge detail.

Don't worry if the sheets are slightly different sizes: this all adds to the creative look of the finished item. Place lace or ribbon loops evenly along the inside edge; these can either be sewn on top or inserted between the layers of the sandwich to give a neater appearance. These are then used to fasten the book pages together.

TIP

If you choose to machine stitch the pages, you need to consider the color of the top thread and the bottom bobbin as both will be seen. The stitch style is up to you.

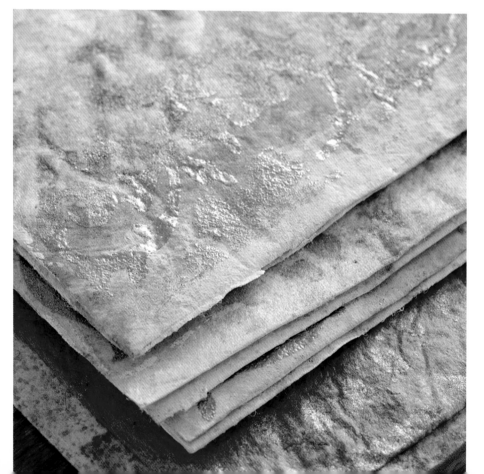

Books of silk paper samples allow you to combine favorite decorative techniques.

# THE MEDIUM METHOD

In the iron method, silk paper is made from fibers that contain the gum sericin, which is activated by heat and moisture. In the medium method, silk that has had the gummy sericin removed is used. This is because the method reintroduces glue to bind the fibers together. Glues that may be used are PVA, marvin medium, and acrylic medium, all of which have a variety of finishes. The glue used for the project shown opposite was an acrylic medium with a matte finish, although you can use glue with another finish, such as satin and gloss. Should you wish, these mediums can also be tinted with acrylic color or metallic flakes. None of the projects in this section had colors added to the medium, which was diluted to approximately one part medium to five parts water (a 1:5 ratio). The strength of the bonding medium should be determined by its final use: if you are making a bag from the silk fabric created, you will need a stronger mix because the bag will be handled. A weaker mix will suffice for a more decorative piece.

Both naturally colored and dyed silks can be used for this method. If using dyed silks, you may find that there is a small leaching of dye color into the medium mix. In my experience, this does not affect the outcome of the piece: just be aware that this slight discoloration might happen.

## SAFETY:

Wash your hands with hot, soapy water if
you get any kind of medium on your hands.

### YOU WILL NEED:

- 2 pieces of lightweight lint-free cloth,
  cut to size

- shallow plastic tray

- dyed silk top or other gum-out fibers

- hot water (just off the boil)

- large spoon

- large bowl or jug for the 1:5
  ratio medium

1 Place the cloth on the bottom of the shallow tray. Pull out fibers from the tops and lay in a north–south direction. The pulls of silk should slightly overlap like roof tiles. Leave a narrow border between the fibers and the edge of the tray.

2 Lay a second layer of silk at right angles to the first layer, again slightly overlapping like roof tiles.

3 Place a second piece of cloth over the silk layers.

4 Pour enough nearly boiling water over the cloth just to wet the fibers. Take care when doing this.

**5** Using the back of the spoon, carefully burnish the surface of the fiber sandwich. This process allows you to spread the water evenly, distributing it throughout the fiber layers. You may need to add a little more water, but don't worry if you seem to have too much as you can pour any excess away. Burnishing helps the fibers to connect using any residue of sericin. If you left the silk layers to dry out at this stage they would bind together, but it would be an extremely fragile connection because these fibers have had most of their sericin removed.

**6** When the water has cooled, roll up the sandwich of fibers and submerge it into medium mix.

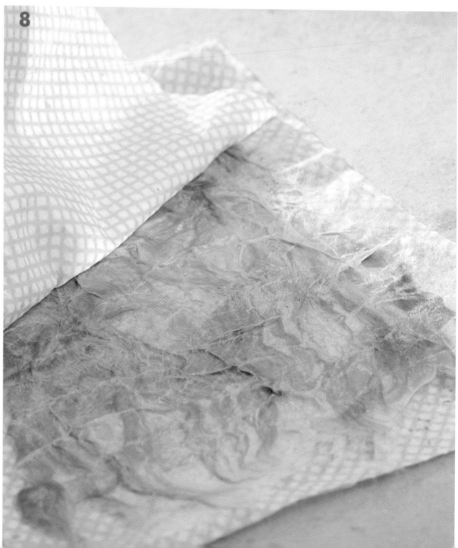

**7** Squash the roll to pump the medium throughout the fiber bundle.

**8** Squeeze out as much of the medium as you can, even out the roll, and open out the fiber sandwich.

**9** At this point, you can leave the piece you have created to dry as it is or fold over the edges as shown here. Whichever you choose to do, cover the fibers again and place the sandwich back into the medium for one final soaking.

**10** Squeeze out any excess medium and unwrap. Allow the silk paper to dry before use.

**Right** The silk rectangle made on pages 70 to 73 with dyed silk tops has a highly textured surface. By placing it on a background of paper made using the iron method, the contrast is enhanced. The spirals were cut from flat, iron method silk paper, and attached with a free motion embroidery pattern of freely drawn spirals. A hint of color was painted on the edge of the spirals so they look as though they are subtly lifting from the surface.

## TYPES OF SILK THAT CAN BE USED IN THE MEDIUM METHOD

mulberry (white) tops

tussah (honey-colored) tops

throwster's waste

condenser waste

split carrier rods

filament

noil variants

# Random texture

In this example, you can see the effect of using a variety of natural, undyed fibers laid out randomly. Highly textured surfaces can be created using this process.

1  Lay out the silk fibers: these do not have to be aligned so long as they overlap and connect. However, aligning fibers will create a stronger fabric. Follow Steps 1 to 4 on page 71, omit Step 5, then continue to the end.

2  By omitting the burnishing step, the end result will be much more textured. After scrunching to remove the excess medium, the fabric can be left to dry naturally, in which case the texture will be very prominent. Alternatively, it can be gently flattened by hand to reduce the height of the texture. It can also be ironed in places to create a contrast of texture.

**Above** Soft textures are created with dyed throwster's waste, resulting in a delicate, open structure.

**Right** This image shows fibers contrasting in both color and texture.

The textured silk background (made on page 75) is an ideal support for natural urchin spines. Simple hand stitching with linen thread emphasizes the contrasting textures.

# Manipulating fibers

The samples on these pages were made by layering loose silk fibers that had been soaked in a medium onto dyed wet-strength tissue. This tissue is known by various names, including repair tissue and bookbinders' tissue, and has properties that are very useful to textile makers. It absorbs color and remains very strong when wet, rather like a fine fabric. When dry, it retains the crispness of paper, and can be folded neatly. If the surface is scrunched up, rolled, and generally softened, it will have the qualities of a draping fabric. It is lightweight and can be stitched and over-colored.

The technique is a little messy, but very rewarding. Place your chosen fibers directly into a bowl of medium. Wearing rubber or latex gloves, squish and squash the fibers until they are saturated. Remove the fibers from the bowl, squeezing out the excess medium, then open and tease them into shapes. Arrange the fibers on the dyed wet-strength tissue; you can move the fibers around until the medium begins to dry out. When dry, another layer of silk fibers can be added and again allowed to dry thoroughly. Please note that if you make a very deep surface using this method the drying time will be considerable. Layered surfaces can be made to a reasonable height, but layering does take quite a while (several days) and patience!

Dyed silk tops soaked in medium were pulled out into free form organic shapes then laid on a dyed wet-strength tissue background.

**Below** A combination of dyed throwster's waste and condenser waste was laid out on dyed wet-strength tissue. This was further adorned with commercially cut, glittered flower shapes, attached by free machining onto the textured surface. Iridescent glass flower beads complete the panel.

Here, dyed silk noil was soaked and laid out on dyed wet-strength tissue before being embellished with stitch method flowers with antique button beads in their centers.

# Casting with a block

Casting on a block is messier than the molding method shown on page 50, but it is fun and the results are worthwhile. In the iron method, gummy fibers are used, which results in a smooth surface to the embossed paper. In this casting method, non-gummy fibers soaked in a medium are employed, which gives the paper far more texture.

The process is a variation on the medium method and works most efficiently with short-fibered silks such as noils. You may wish to try casting with other fibers, but the results will vary.

Wearing rubber or latex gloves, plunge the noil fibers into a concentrated medium. Squish and squash them until they are saturated,

then lift the fibers and squeeze out the excess medium. Open out the noil fiber mass and spread it into thin layers on top of a deeply etched molding block. Press the fibers into the mold. If holes appear in the silk layer, either add more saturated fibers or just accept the holes and see them as a creative bonus.

Turn over the molding block onto a plastic-covered surface and press down to compact and consolidate the silk cast. Remove the cast by teasing it away from the molding block and lay the silk cast aside to dry. At this stage you can create a 3-D piece. Place the cast over a suitable object, such as a plastic cup, and when the cast is dry it will take the shape of that object. To make a flat piece, lay out the cast silk on a flat surface.

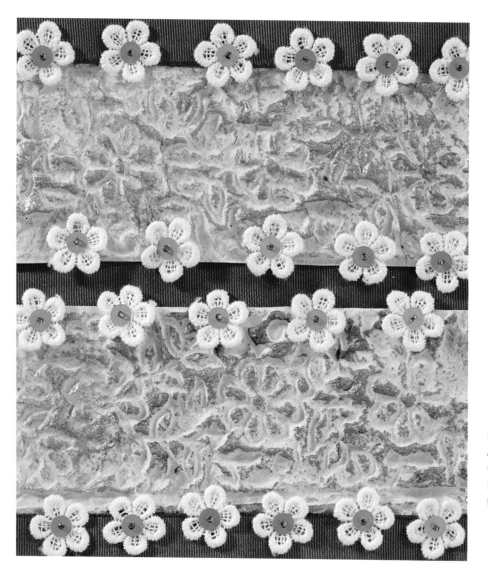

**Left** In this sample I enhanced the casts with a fine layer of acrylic paint and used small flowers to attach them to a fabric background. Each flower was stitched through with a sequin and a bead.

It is important to remove the silk cast immediately from the molding block, as it will adhere if allowed to dry. When dry, the silk cast can be painted or enhanced with patinating waxes. The cast pieces can be used as art works in their own right or cut out and attached to other textile surfaces with glue or stitches.

## NOIL FIBERS

The samples on pages 80 to 83 were made with noil. There are two kinds: tussah noil is a golden colored fiber that can be natural or dyed; clean, bleached noil is a whiter fiber that is also available in natural or dyed form. See page 126 for more on noil.

# Creating texture with an iron

A wide selection of silk types is used in this method of making a textured surface. The larger the "palette" of silks you have, the greater the decorative possibilities. Although the effect is seen more easily using natural tones, such as the ones used here, combinations of colored and natural fibers or colored fibers only can be used.

Make a sheet of silk paper using the medium method and leave to dry. Cover the areas to be ironed with a piece of silicone or greaseproof paper and, with the iron on the hottest setting, press down and smooth over the area you want to "shine." This takes only a moment so don't linger on any area. Small travel irons are best as they have a smaller area than ordinary domestic irons. Hoof irons or quilting irons are even smaller, making them useful for this process. Papers treated to smoothing can be further embellished with matt and shiny threads.

This technique can be used to create considerable contrast or more subtle and elegant pieces. If you use mulberry and tussah tops, you will notice that the ironed areas will really shine and shimmer in contrast to areas that are left un-ironed. Areas on your design that have shorter more textured silk areas will be smoothed and offer a contrast of texture.

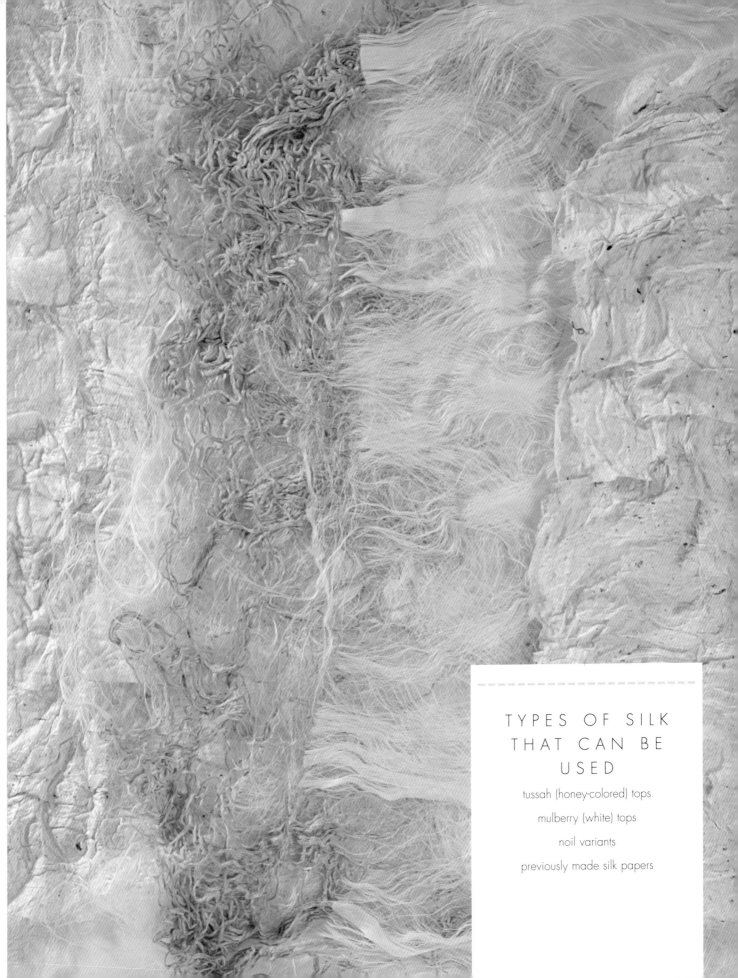

## TYPES OF SILK THAT CAN BE USED

tussah (honey-colored) tops

mulberry (white) tops

noil variants

previously made silk papers

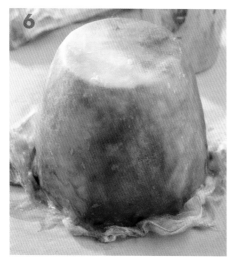

**6** When you are happy with the thickness of the bowl, cover with a final layer of glue.

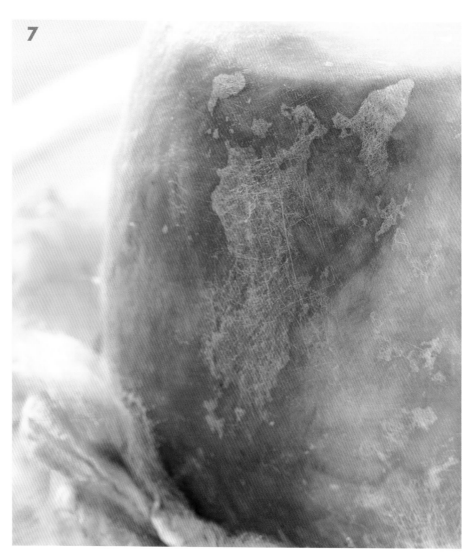

**7** Apply glue until there are no dry patches left. Do not worry about the dry bottom edge: this will be cut off after the silk cast has dried. The completed cast should be left to dry in a warm environment. Depending on how many layers and the ambient temperature of the drying place, this can take one or more days.

**8** When the silk cast is completely dry, gently ease the shape off the mold. Slip a flat knife in between the plastic wrap and the silk cast and run the blade around the mold, or, if you are brave, simply peel the cast away. The cast is easily reshaped and generally returns to its original state.

### TIP

Choose a mold that will allow for easy removal of the cast. If you choose a mold with an intricate shape, the cast can be cut down in order to remove it and then re-pasted to create a whole shape. This is quite difficult to achieve so, until you have gained experience in this method, I would strongly recommend the use of a gently tapering mold, such as a vase or a small basin.

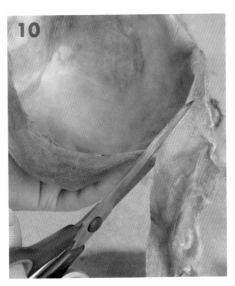

9 With a ruler and a pen, measure and mark a line along the top where you want to remove the excess from the cast.

10 Using a sharp pair of long-bladed scissors, cut decisively along the marked line. If small-bladed scissors are used, a smooth cut line will be difficult to achieve.

11 At this stage, you can add a small amount of sealant (either more cellulose paste or acrylic medium, depending on what you used) or some acrylic paint to the cut edge to seal it. Alternatively, it can be left as it is. I finished the edge of the bowl with individual leaves made using the stitched method described on page 94. The veins of each leaf were defined with machine stitches before each piece was stitched on by hand.

**Left** This vessel was molded around a jelly jar. The rim clearly shows the natural rippling of the edges of the mawata hankies from which the bowl was made. The body of the bowl has been enhanced with an undulating machine-stitched line that complements the ripple of the edge.

**Opposite** The edge of this delicate bowl was cut away to neaten it, then decorated with machine zigzag stitch and beads.

# THE STITCHED METHOD

A beautiful fabric can be created from silk fibers by using free-motion embroidery combined with water-soluble film. Pre-programmed or free-motion embroidery allows a delicate filigree of loose silk fibers to be connected, whatever their form. Free-motion embroidery requires three changes to the set up of your machine. Refer to your manual when changing settings, as each machine has its own set up parameters. Many people feel that they can use a bare needle. This is dangerous as a moment's distraction can cause injury and machines are designed to form the stitch properly when a foot is attached.

The type of water-soluble film used in this method is a self-supporting film that requires no further stabilization. This means that you should not need a frame to control the movement of the silk sandwich as you work. The film is generally sold under the trade name Romeo, but is available under other names, and is designed to work in a wide range of climate conditions. It is a heavyweight transparent film that remains inert until soaked in water. It does not have a top surface and either side can be used. Some films have a sticky feel in very humid climatic conditions but this should not affect their function. Check with your local craft suppliers and always read the manufacturer's instructions if in doubt.

## THE STITCHED METHOD

## SAFETY:

The feed dog must be lowered or covered, and it is essential that the appropriate free-motion foot is attached. It is very dangerous to sew without a foot attached, and the stitches will be formed incorrectly.

## YOU WILL NEED:

- 1 sheet of Romeo water-soluble material or equivalent film
- dyed hankie
- dyed silk tops
- sewing machine
- threads—cotton, synthetic, or silk
- black marker pen
- ruler
- scissors

1 Most water-soluble films are folded over, so they first need to be opened up. If you have a product that is a single sheet, you will need two pieces about the same size. Select your silk fibers. I chose a dyed hankie split into quite thin layers, and silk tops in a contrasting color. Don't worry about over-lapping the hankies, as it makes little difference to the thickness of the layers. Fold over the top layer of water-soluble film to make a silk sandwich.

2 Set your machine to free motion mode—no feed dogs, no stitch length or stitch width. Sew across the silk sandwich in a gentle looping motion to create an interlocking structure.

3 With a marker pen, draw out a square 6 x 6 in. (15 x 15 cm) and cut out.

4 Keep the off-cuts for use in another project.

TIP

You can use a different color thread or, indeed, thickness of thread on the bottom bobbin to that of the top thread, as your work may be seen from both sides.

**5** Place the newly created fabric into a bowl of warm water and allow it to soak for about twenty minutes. It is at this stage that the water-soluble film will dissolve and dissipate from the fabric into the water. You may need to repeat this process to remove all the water-soluble film. The film will become gelatinous and dissolve in the water, which will go cloudy.

**6** Allow the silk square to dry out on a paper towel. If you wish, you can iron the dried fabric flat or leave it un-ironed for an interesting, irregular texture.

**Right** I transformed the silk paper square into this dainty container by cutting a second square of silk fabric the same size as the first, folding over the corners, and then sewing the edges together to create a container. I overlaid tight satin stitches and looser zigzag stitches to create an interesting effect. Finally, I edged the corner triangles with beads.

To create this tiara, I placed a combination of dyed silk hankies and silk tops between two sheets of water-soluble film. After drawing on the outline of a tiara, I filled in the shape with matching thread, using free motion embroidery. When the film had dissolved, I sewed the stitched piece onto a lightweight Vilene backing and embellished it with twinkling gems and gold beads

# Making a scarf

Creating larger items, such these scarves, requires a little more preparation than for a small piece made from the stitch method. When laying out the fibers, give some thought to the color, texture, and shape of the final item. You may wish to use various silk fibers in a single color throughout, or use two colors: one on the bottom layer and one on the top so that the scarf will be a different color on each side. Color could also flow from one end to the other either randomly, or be laid out in a controlled, graduated manner.

A long slim scarf with rounded ends is a simple shape to start with, but you can choose more innovative shapes. Cut out wavy or curled shapes from spare fabric to see how the finished scarf will drape or fall around your neck. Use this as your template. The length is dependent on personal preference: measure a favorite scarf to get an idea of the length you need. Using different threads on the top and bottom bobbin will create color variation. You should also consider the stitch you are going to use. A dense stitch pattern will create a stiffer result than an open, lace-like stitch pattern, which will give the finished scarf a more fluid drape.

Draw around the template onto water-soluble fabric with a marker pen. Remove the template and save it for future projects. Hand tack around the edges to secure the layers together with large bold stitches. Alternatively, there are temporary adhesives (especially created for textile artists) that dissolve with the water-soluble film. When the layers are complete and secure, roll up the sandwich so that you have about 8 in. (20 cm) available to stitch on. Stich this area, then open up the roll to expose more unstitched area. As you progress, the stitched area can be rolled up to make it easier to manipulate.

When the body of the scarf has been fully stitched, open out the roll and consider the edges. A simple zigzag or satin stitch sewn around the perimeter of the scarf is a simple way to bind the edges or create a selvedge. Make a sample to test the effect before starting on the scarf edges. (If the edge stitching is too tight or dense, this will affect the drape of the scarf.) When the stitching is complete, dissolve the water-soluble film as described on page 98 and leave to dry.

The addition of beads and stitched dangles or indeed any embellishment will personalize your piece. Adding beads to the ends of your scarf will help it hang better when worn.

# Making jewelry

Small pieces of silk paper made using the stitched method can be further embellished and transformed into exciting pieces of jewelry. To create these necklaces, make up as many stitched shapes as you desire for your necklace. Trace around the templates (see page 124) onto water-soluble film and stitch within the shapes. Make the units in pairs (back and front) or folded.

Rows of concentric stitching on the circular shapes will makes the final pieces slightly elastic and so make padding them easier. On larger circles concentric stitching works equally well, but small overlapping squiggles give a more organic effect. Cut light-weight craft felt or other appropriate material just smaller than the unit and use several layers, each smaller than the other, to give a domed effect to the jewelry. Stitch the units together by hand using appropriately colored thread. Use a ladder stitch to create a firm edge; if a slip stitch is used to bind over the edge, the result will be softer. A machine zigzag stitch can be used, but mind your fingers because the pieces will be quite small. The completed units can be stitched together with beads, or lay cording between the elements as you stitch. Enhance the units with small seed beads or other decorative elements.

## TIP

The combination of color, texture, and stitch marks is very important for these small jewelry items: all the elements should work well together to create a harmonious ensemble for you to wear.

# Using pre-programmed stitches

Take a good look at your sewing machine manual to familiarize yourself with the many ways that the machine can be pre-programmed to create stitch patterns. Don't be put off if you have an older or a more basic machine: utilitarian stitches, such as blind hemming, zigzag and buttonhole can be used in a very creative and decorative manner. Unique surfaces can be achieved by sewing stitches very close together, by overlaying them, or by using a variety of shiny metallic or variegated threads.

The easy way to use pre-programmed stitches to create a piece of silk paper is to choose the default pattern that the machine uses without human intervention. Before stitching onto silk fibers, carry out a test on a trial cloth: by altering the stitch width and length many variations can be achieved. Remember that the purpose behind the stitching is to connect the silk fibers between the interlocking stitches. Follow the instructions for the stitched method on pages 96 to 98.

To make a handy evening bag, create a number of squares using pre-programmed stitches, with zigzag stitches around the edges to form individual units. A bag can then be constructed by linking these squares together (see template page 124). Hand stitching is a lovely final adornment to the surface.

## TIP

It is always a good idea to read your sewing machine manual every now and again. I nearly always discover something that I had forgotten, and find inspiration in revisiting the more simple stitch patterns.

This evening bag was made out of sixteen squares, each of which was embellished with different pre-programed stitches. When the squares were completed, I removed the water-soluble film and hand stitched the bag together.

# Making a stitched vessel

This vessel may look complex, but it is actually constructed from a rectangle and a circle then manipulated into a more free-form shape by tucking and pleating. You will need a dyed silk cap, some dyed throwster, and a compass or circular object to draw around in addition to the materials listed on page 96. If you want to create a delicate vessel, use thin layers of silk cap. If you require a more robust or solid structure, add more layers of silk at the stage of assembling the silk sandwich.

Stretch a silk cap and lay it out on a sheet of water-soluble film, filling in any thin areas. (Regardless of the density of the fabric you want to create, even layers are better than uneven layers.) Distribute some throwster's waste over the cap to add drama to the surface. Fold over the water-soluble film and draw a rectangle and circle on it with a marker pen. Outline the edges of these shapes with a free motion straight stitch. This will give you a stronger, more resilient edge that will provide a consistent and non-distorting shape when the vessel is assembled. Stitch the rectangle and circle in free motion stitch pattern of your choice.

When the pieces are completely stitched, cut them out and leave a tiny margin to the edge of the stitch lines. Using a zigzag or satin stitch to bind the stitches over will strengthen and form a selvedge to make the construction easier. Dissolve the water-soluble film and leave the shapes to dry. When, dry iron them flat then assemble the vessel with a machine stitch or by hand. To create the freeform shape, make a tuck, and use a running stitch to secure it.

## TIP

If you want to line your vessel, copy the original template but allow an extra margin all around. Assemble and use a small catch or slip edge to secure the lining to the inner edge of the vessel. If you decide not to line it, use variegated thread on the bobbin so, when the vessel is made up, there will be a quirky color mix visible on the inside. Alternatively, use a contrasting color to add drama to the piece.

# Hydrangea panels

An artistic combination of silk paper methods was employed to create these pieces. I began by printing onto pieces of iron method silk paper with a stamp made from compacted polystyrene packaging cut into a small rectangle and glued to a cardboard backing. The image was incised into the surface of the polystyrene with a stylus. A more permanent block can be made from lino or printers' rubber, but this will take longer to create. The stamped pieces were set aside.

I loosely stitched together some dyed silk fibers following the stitched method. I then cut up the stitched sheet and rewove the strips before adding free-motion stitches over the new structure. This was then soaked to remove the water-soluble film, left to dry, then set aside.

Another key element in these panels is iron method paper (pages 32 to 67) with naturally dried out hydrangea flowers incorporated into it. Once the various elements had been assembled, it was time to arrange them and stitch them together. In a collage like this, the balance of the piece should be borne in mind. Use paper pieces to practice your arrangement before you commit to sewing down the silk elements. My hydrangea panels were further adorned with more free-motion stitching across the surface. Free-motion flowers and patched slips (a slip is a separate element added to the main piece) were dotted around the surface to create a harmonious composition.

Strips of stitched method silk fabric were woven together and restitched before the water-soluble stabilizer was removed.

**Left** Detail of free-motion hydrangea flowers made from sheer fabric.

TIP

If you want to create an iron method paper with petal inclusions, choose a flower that is not too fleshy. When these flowers are dried out, they may not give a wholly satisfactory result. Flowers such as roses (petals only) lobelia, pansies, and violets dry well and still retain some color.

# WEAVING AND OVERDYEING RODS

This chapter demonstrates some of the ways in which rods and cocoons can be used to create decorative pieces with a strong structural element by cutting, slicing, overdyeing, inserting, and painting them. Working with these rigid structures is very different to working with the fibers used in previous chapters. Using rods and cocoons, both whole and cut, allows the structural character to remain, even when stretched and (in the case of rods) twisted. As the photograph opposite shows, dyed and stretched rods make an attractive panel. Cocoons particularly come into their own when used for jewelry, giving an ageless elegance and durability to any design.

# Weaving and overdyeing

When you separate layers from dyed rods, the areas of dye penetration will be revealed. If you discover areas that are undyed, there are several options available to you: one is to accept and embrace these undyed areas within your work! Alternatively, you can go over the undyed areas with textile paint, simply letting the paint dry (if the piece will be used for decorative purposes only ) or fixing it by following the manufacturer's instructions. My favorite approach is to paint the undyed areas

with acid dyes, using a sponge brush (see page 24) to spot color certain areas or by total immersion. Rather nice color combinations can be achieved by overdyeing the rod slivers completely.

In this sample, I created a woven background using rods and decorative elements that were edged with machine stitching. The piece shows the subtlety of color that can be achieved by dyeing then overdyeing rods. I separated selected rods then wove them together to form a sheet of silk. I supported the

loosely woven structure by placing it on a lightweight Vilene backing. This allowed me to control the structure and stitch over the surface more efficiently. I added stitched elements to the surface to reinforce the block-and-line surface of the silk panel background. You may wish to cut the rod layers along their length and weave them over the rest to create a more intricate woven fabric. Leave the joins exposed or hide them under the woven layers, as you prefer.

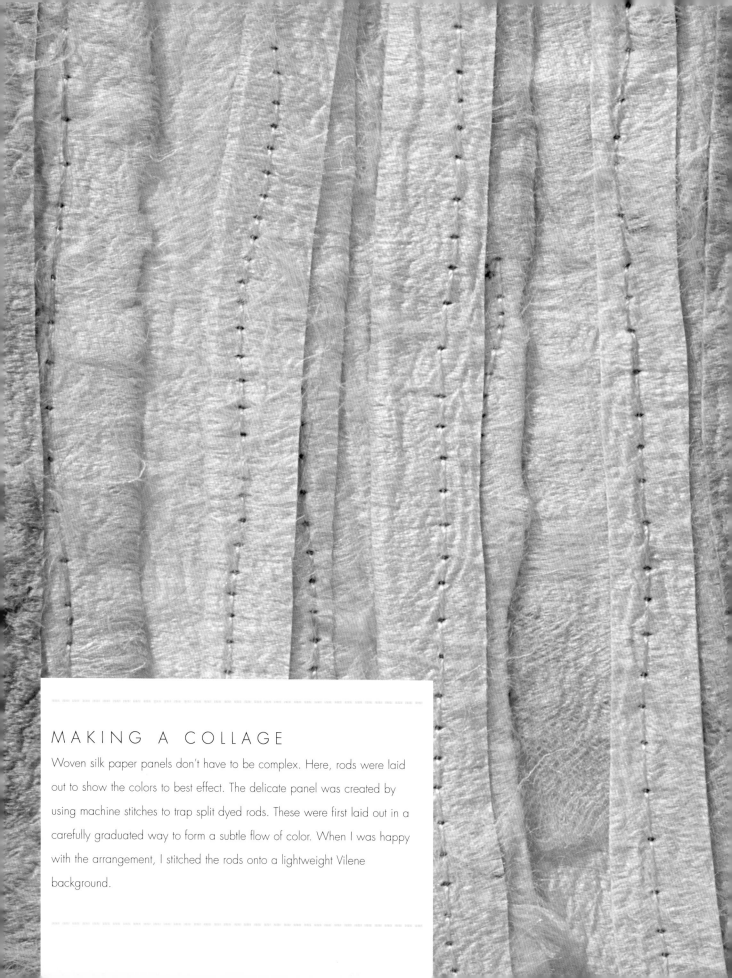

## MAKING A COLLAGE

Woven silk paper panels don't have to be complex. Here, rods were laid out to show the colors to best effect. The delicate panel was created by using machine stitches to trap split dyed rods. These were first laid out in a carefully graduated way to form a subtle flow of color. When I was happy with the arrangement, I stitched the rods onto a lightweight Vilene background.

# Creating roses

To create these charming flowers, select at least three rods for each rose you wish to create. Process each rod to give you a number of layers following the method shown on page 14. From these separated layers, select those whose color is most appropriate for the centers (the bud) and those that are more suited for the faded petals of the outside of the rose. Curl back each layer so that the heart of the rose has an outward curve. Stitch the rose together at the base of the bud then attach the outer petals. You will find that each layer from a rod will stretch quite considerably and may even start to twist naturally on itself to form a rosette with barely any effort on your part. Stitch the stretched-out layer to the base of the bud, adding more layers until the flower is to your liking. A large, dramatic tea rose can be achieved by attaching the bud and basic rose shape to a fabric backing, then stitching more rods to that background to create a larger flower head.

## TIP

For a more natural effect, the rods can be dyed to rose-like colors. The "roses" can be enhanced further by inserting fringes in between the layers as they are made, and you can create "dew" by adding a drop or two of a clear-drying glue to the edges.

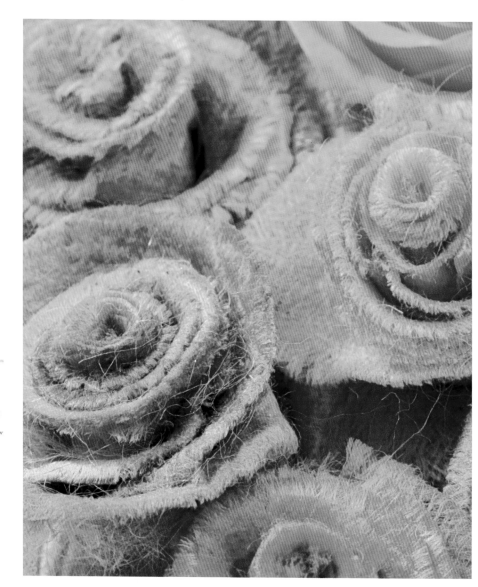

# Making vessels

These decorative containers are made from overdyed silk rods that were first split and laid onto a lightweight Vilene backing. I used free-motion embroidery to attach the rod slivers to the backing to create a sheet of fabric. From this I cut four rectangles approximately 3 x 7 in. (7.5 x 18 cm) and a base piece 3 in. (8 cm) square. I lined each of these pieces, attaching the lining by using a zigzag stitch around the edges. Finally, I assembled the containers with hand stitches and edged the joins with beads.

# Decorative panels

Whether dyed or natural, split cocoons arranged on a sympathetic background make unusual panels that look great framed and hung on a wall or displayed flat on a table. In the orange sample (opposite), dyed whole cocoons were cut in half, arranged in rows—cut side down—and stitched down onto a fabric background to create a striking decorative panel. Blue beads were chosen to accent the bright orange dye.

**Right** Silk paper made using the medium method was cut, stitched, and decorated with half cocoons and buttons.

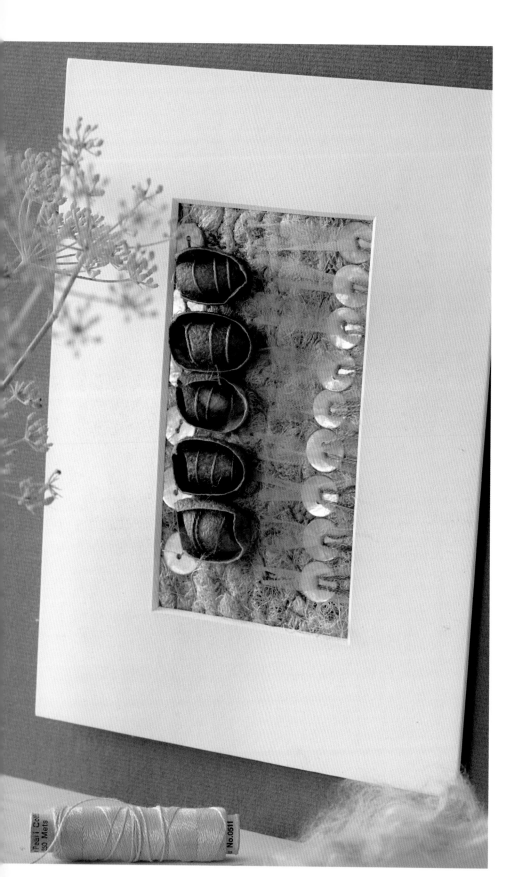

**Left** This decorative panel uses laterally sliced, whole cocoons which have been placed inside each other and stitched down. The silk paper background is detailed further with mother-of-pearl discs and sheer yarn-thread stitchery.

**Top left (opposite)** Here, dyed, cut cocoons were stitched with contrasting thread to create organic form.

**Top right (opposite)** Sliced, cut cocoons, together with variegated thread, create a limpet-like surface.

**Bottom right (opposite)** In this example, whole cocoons were sliced laterally and painted with metallic textile paint on the outside and metal flake on the inside. They were then connected with linen cord and threaded with beads for detailing.

**Bottom left (opposite)** Whole cocoons and smaller cut cocoons were sliced and placed inside each other to create delicate porcelain-like structures.

# Templates

Enlarge the templates to suit your designs. Copy the Hydrangea and Necklace templates onto cardstock, lay the templates onto silk paper and draw around the shapes with a fine pencil. Draw the Booklet pattern directly onto a sheet of silk paper using a soft pencil and ruler. The Evening Bag pattern shows how seventeen silk paper squares can be sewn together and folded to create a purse.

### p.42, Hydrangea

Fold all petals along the fold lines, crease and unfold. Fold one petal in again. Rotate the flower clockwise and fold the next petal in. As you fold the third petal, gently lift the lobe of the first petal to allow the third to slip underneath. Fold the fourth petal, again lifting the first petal to interlock all four petals.

### p.102-103, Necklaces

Follow the instructions on page 102 to make up the two necklaces. The diamond and large circle are folded in half and padded, whereas the small circle is doubled up and padded.

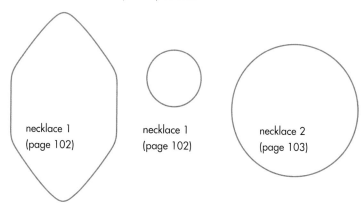

necklace 1
(page 102)

necklace 1
(page 102)

necklace 2
(page 103)

### p.64, Booklet

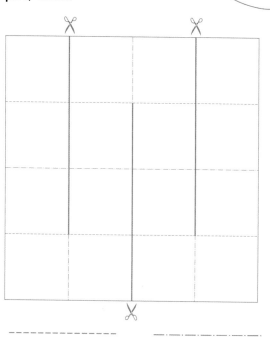

Key for valley fold       Key for mountain fold

### p.104, Evening Bag

Sew side A to A, B to B, etc., leaving the short outer edges unsewn. Fold up a rectangle in the center to form the base of the bag.

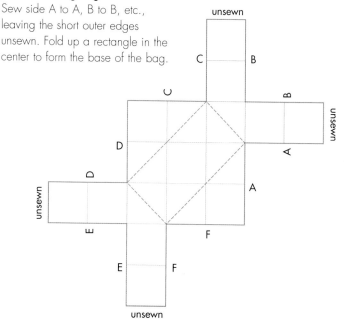

# Suppliers

Silk fibers are not available from general craft stores, but there are a number of companies worldwide who supply them. All the suppliers listed here are knowledgeable, carry a wide variety of silk fiber and related products, and will despatch fibers to customers.

*Craftynotions is owned and run by Sarah Lawrence and ships worldwide. The company stocks all the products used in this book. Creative Colour Sprays are a Craftynotions brand product but similar products are available from other sources.*

## Canvas

Linnégatan 57
413 08 GÖTEBORG
Sweden
www.canvasshop.se
*Carries a wide range of dyed and undyed silk fibers as well as many other items used within the book.*

## Craftynotions Ltd.

Unit 2 Jessop Way
Newark NG24 2ER
United Kingdom
www.craftynotions.com

## Joggles.com, LLC

1454 Main Street Unit 30
West Warwick, RI
USA
www.joggles.com
*Supplier of dyed and undyed silk fibers*

## Rainbow Silks

6 Wheelers Yard,
Great Missenden HP16 0AL
United Kingdom
www.rainbowsilks.co.uk
*Supplies dyed and undyed silk fibers*

## The Silk Route

Cross Cottage,
Cross Lane
Frimley Green
GU16 6LN, UK
www.thesilkroute.co.uk
*Specialist in silk threads and fabrics*

## The Thread Studio

6 Smith Street
Perth
Western Australia
www.thethreadstudio.com
*Stocks a wide range of dyed and undyed silk fibers, and related materials.*

## Treenway Silks

501 Musgrave Road
Salt Spring Island
British Columbia, V8K 1V5
Canada
www.treenwaysilks.com
*Stocks dyed and undyed silk fibers*

# Glossary

## BELL

A bell is formed from many silk caps stretched over a single form. A bell may contain up to 1,500 stretched cocoons.

## BOMBYX MORI

The silk moth that feeds on mulberry leaves and produces a fine, lustrous filament.

## CARDING

The process of combing fibers into alignment.

## CARRIER ROD

Guide bar over which the silk is drawn in the process of reeling the silk. Waste silk builds up on this bar and is periodically removed by slitting.

## COCOON

A silk cocoon is the result of the process undertaken by the silk worm to create a protective environment while it pupates from a larva to a moth.

## COCOON STRIPPINGS

Silk waste from the outer layers of the cocoon which still contains the sericin.

## CONDENSER WASTE

Silk condenser waste looks like unspun yarn. The fibers are easily separated.

## DEGUMMING

The process of removing the sericin from the silk fiber.

## DUPION

A fabric woven from conjoined cocoons.

## FIBRION

The inert protein fiber created by silk worms, which is covered with sericin.

## FILAMENT

An individual strand of silk which may

*Hankie*

vary in length from around 450 yards to a remarkable 2,000 yards.

## HANKIE

Cocoon that has been softened and stretched to form a square shape similar in size to a lady's handkerchief.

## MAWATA CAPS

Softened cocoons that are stretched over a bell-shaped form (see Bell).

*Carrier rods*

*Cocoon strippings*

*Mawata caps*

## MULBERRY

Refers to the white or common mulberry bush (*Morus alba*), a small deciduous tree native to China, which is the sole food of the *Bombyx mori* silk worm. Hence, mulberry silk.

## NOIL

Short fibers that are created when producing a spun silk fiber. Noil fibers are very light and come in a bulky fibrous mass.

## RAW SILK

Silk that has been taken from the cocoon but still has the sericin remaining.

## SERICIN

The gum surrounding the fibrion fiber, which hardens on contact with air, allowing the silk worm to produce its cocoon.

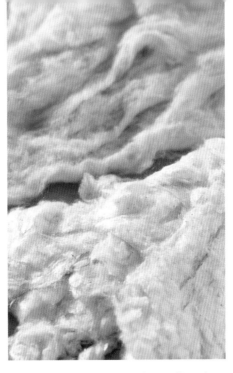

*Tussah silk noil (top) and clean silk noil*

## SILK

The product secreted by spinerettes located on the head of the silk worm. This hardens on contact with air and is composed of fibrion and sericin.

## SILK SLIVER

Lengths of sliver are thinner than silk tops and only slightly twisted.

## SILK TOP

Broken fibers produced by the cleaning and carding processes. The fibers remain aligned to form a continuous sliver typically used in the spinning process.

## THROWING

The process of creating a silk thread from filament by winding, doubling, and twisting.

## THROWSTER'S WASTE

Residue from the process of "throwing," which is the formation of silk thread.

## TUSSAH SILK

Silk from worms that are not *Bombyx mori* and therefore not fed on mulberry. Tussah is found in many colors from honey to deep caramel. It tends to be less lustrous than mulberry silk.

*Silk*

*Gummy throwster's waste (top) and degummed throwster's waste*

*Tussah silk sliver (top) and mulberry silk sliver*

128

# Index

As many materials and techniques are used throughout the book, the page references are intended to direct the reader to substantial entries only. Page numbers in *italics* refer to illustrations.

**AUTHOR'S ACKNOWLEDGMENTS**

I would like to thank Fran Lawrence for her nimble typing fingers and tolerance of a middle-aged mother; the team at craftynotions.com, and my friend Christine. Thanks also to Janet at Breslich & Foss (and her dog Houdi) for her help, guidance and—above all—patience.